The Surprised Medium

Cheryn Ryan

The Surprised Medium

Copyright © 2021 Cheryn Ryan
Cover art © Ian Andreiev
ID 97070641 Dreamstime.com

www.cherynryan.com

All rights reserved. No part of this book may be reproduced or transmitted, in any form, or by any means, electronic or mechanical, including photocopying, recording copying, or by any information storage and retrieval system, without the written permission of the author or her legal representative, except where permitted by law.

The author makes no guarantee or warranties, with respect to another person utilizing or following the strategy of the author's personal spiritual offerings. Some persons names and occurrences have been changed for privacy. This book is sold with the understanding the author has personal beliefs and experiences, which she shares with love and gratitude.

Library of Congress Control Number: 2021906894

ISBN-978-1-7333044-1-2 (Paperback)

Cheryn Ryan

Many Thanks to…

Carl - Always and Forever,

I love you and thank you for being my "One and Only".

Michelle, Peg, Jane, Judith, and Ryan, Thank you for your continued encouragement and love.

Karuna and Kohei, Please Know This -- You have my everlasting and eternal heart.

Deanna, Linda, and Connie, You are brave women. I love you, and appreciate your sharing.

And to my loved ones in Heaven:

Christy, Christine, Clifford, Anna Lee, Tea, Al and Phyllis, Thanks for your guidance, love, and messages. *I'll see ya!*

Special Thanks to:

Formatting & Editing Guru:
Larry Morris @ larrymorrisbooks.com

Photographer & Cheerleader: Peg Shafer

Mediums:

Linda Drake @ lindadrakeconsulting.com;
Suzanne Giesemann @ suzannegiesemann.com;
Mavis Pitilla @ mavispitilla.com;
John Edward @ johnedward.net

Also by Cheryn Ryan:

RSD A Cure for Me

Preface

When she was young, Cheryn thought she was "making up" stories about people she knew, people passing in cars, people in her neighborhood. It turned out, she wasn't creating those stories. Fast forward into adulthood, Cheryn experienced more and more messages from her loved ones. She had premonitions, dreams, warnings of danger, and real-time visions. However, she didn't realize she could receive similar information for other people, until she attended a seminar on Mediumship. It was at that workshop, she heard, saw, and felt a stranger's family in the Next Life, reach out to him -- *through* her!

As an Evidential Medium, Cheryn helps soothe the hearts of people grieving losses of their loved ones. She knows her real clients are those loving Spirit People, who work hard to share their thoughts, feelings, visions, and messages through people like Cheryn, The Surprised Medium

Go ahead ... *ask me.*

Ask me if, when I was planning my life, I ever, *EVER* thought about becoming a Professional Medium. My answer would have been,

"NO! ... Are you CRAZY?"

However, today I **am** a Medium.

I serve Holy Spirit.

It is an honor ... beyond words.

I receive messages from the after-life and give that information to the *"Walking Wounded"* -- people grieving the passing of their loved ones.

It is my privilege to see, hear, and feel these memories, words, and emotions being relayed, through me, and to help ease their pain. I know of this pain, I feel this pain.

I have a beautiful daughter and many, many loved ones alive in Heaven (the name given to the after-life during historical times, and still used by many religions). I refer to the Next World as Heaven and Spirit World. I refer to our God as Creator, Great Spirit, Holy Spirit, and Great Holy Spirit, and *simply*, God. My name for those people who have passed: Spirit People, Beloved, Loved Ones, and Spirit.

I've always been psychic, though I did not declare that information to people -- other than my parents for many years. I had numerous lucid dreams and vivid revelations and have been the recipient of many after death communications from my loved ones.

I thought everyone knew what I knew! I was utterly surprised upon discovering my gifts are available for me to share with other people, too. Some of the gifts with which I have been blessed: Claircognizance — I simply "know" something. Clairaudience — I "hear" a familiar phrase, song (*or most often)*, I hear Spirit People and my own Spirit Guides speaking directly to me. Clairvoyance — I "see" memories and faint visions of people and places. Clairsentience — I "feel" emotions and sometimes, injuries and illnesses.

While here, we are all Physical and when we transcend, we are all Spirit.

Angels and Guides are the dedicated helpers for God. They are here to remind us we are a part of the God Consciousness; to nudge us to stay on our highest path and to intervene on our behalf, when we're in trouble or danger.

I am but one, of almost 110 Billion people, who have lived on Earth. I hold no advanced or prestigious degrees. I am a former business owner and Realtor. I am an artist and the author of a book on self-healing; And, because of my experiences, I am here to speak on the truth of our on-going lives. My role on this beautiful planet is to bring wonderful information to anyone who asks, *"Is there life after life?"*

With truth and love,

Cheryn Ryan,

The Surprised Medium

Cheryn Ryan

OH MY GOSH, I'M A MEDIUM!

Some Mediums knew they could commune with unknown Spirit People their whole lives; I'm not one of them. I have dear friends who had knowledge of the connections between here and the Next World when they were children. It took me a bit longer to get that equation right; I now know I have always had the ability to *be* a Medium.

We humans are always on our soul's journey, whether we are aware of it, or not. The spiritual understandings I held as a child changed as I grew older and wiser. I did not leave all the teachings of my youth behind; I'm a Christian and I've learned there are other spiritual belief systems that resonate with the values of Christianity.

I know the Source of All (what I still call God) is within – not "out there, somewhere". I also know there is no location called "Hell". *Heaven and Hell are not locations*, they remain "locations" only in antiquated theological teachings, initially used to control "The People" by those in power.

Our spiritual truths expand, as our human minds and hearts expand; That process continues after our transition. When our human bodies die, our souls go to the SAME vibrational source where we all seek to become wiser and more loving and where we will learn to release those bad practices we had as humans. This happens in order to grow into the souls we are meant to become.

God (Great Holy Spirit, The Source of All) loves us and wants us to evolve into our highest and best potential, where/when we will join the vibrational plane with Great Holy Spirit and help others from the Light of Love. I know this sounds like a fantasy and overly simplistic, but millions upon millions of people believe it's true.

In the meantime, we are here to serve fellow human beings. Our prayers reach our loved ones on a soul level here, and in the next phases of Life Everlasting.

Isaiah 30:21

Whether you turn to the right or to the left, your ears will hear a voice behind you saying:

"This is the way; Walk in it."

God is Everywhere.
We are part of God.

The Surprised Medium

The Beginning of My Mediumship

One day my minister and friend, Ellen told me about an Author and Medium who was scheduled to give a talk at our church. She said the messages this author would bring were "right down my alley". I agreed to attend her talk, and was really glad I did, because this speaker, Suzanne Giesemann, would become one of my favorite teachers.

I attended the meeting and was duly impressed with Suzanne. Her delivery was flawless and her life story was truly incredible. She has a very analytical mind and I couldn't wait to read her book and learn more about her.

Suzanne was an aide to the Joint Chiefs of Staff of the United States of America and was on a flight to Europe with her bosses when the 911 attacks occurred. The plane turned around and was the last one to land on American soil that terrible day.

Suzanne and her husband retired to sail the world, not long after that … *then her life's story gets very, very interesting!*

The Surprised Medium

BETH

It's four months later, and I'm in a large meeting room with two hundred, or more, people. Suzanne Giesemann, Medium and Author, is the featured speaker and teacher during this weekend seminar. The majority of these attendees are driven by curiosity about life after death. Others are here to learn how we might truly help people who are grieving the deaths of loved ones. Actually, *I KNOW* this is true for me and many more.

Three of my friends and I are here with this room full of attentive students, who have been listening to Suzanne talk about Serving Spirit.

Suzanne has been talking for several hours, and the information she shared has been mesmerizing! Then, she tells us it's time for our first "psychic" experiment and we are instructed what to do.

For this exercise we are all told to begin by saying what we "know" about the unseen strangers, who positioned themselves and are silently standing behind some of us and are tapping us on our backs. As I stand facing a wall, I feel that tap on my shoulder...

And, I begin... haltingly, holding back, and thinking,

"Is this a message from Spirit, or is it my imagination overloading? – It must be my imagination!"

I need to run for the closest exit!

"Whoa! What is going on?"

My mind is racing and filling with pictures of a woman with blue eyes and long, curly, blonde hair. She is riding a bike. Uh-oh, I feel very dizzy, and in the next instant, I see mountains and hear windchimes ringing in a breeze! I hear the name "Beth", and I say it out loud.

The Surprised Medium

I don't know what to make of all these random visions, sounds, and feelings, but I start telling these things to whoever is behind me right now.

When time is up, I turn around to see … *Beth, a short woman with long curly blonde hair and beautiful blue eyes!*

She tells me she just moved to this area from *"a mountain top in Colorado and had wind chimes all over her property"*. Then she says she had recently been told by her doctor to ride a bike for *her occasional bouts of vertigo.*

My mouth is wide open and I'm totally amazed by my … *by Spirit's* accuracy!

We break for lunch and my friends, Phyllis, Jane, Judith, Anne, and I decide to go scope out the local landscape during our lunch break. We find a nice Mexican food restaurant and enjoy a lunch, filled with laughter and awe, as we begin re-telling our experiences.

It seems we all had similar bouts of fear, then a recognition that there was *"something"* there during our readings. We all decide to stay, do the work, and attempt to discover more wonders.

I Surrender Ego and Ask for Clarity

The Surprised Medium

Say, "Ray"!

Our instruction after lunch is for half of the attendees to sit in a chair and the other half to grab a chair and set it down in front of someone who is waiting for them, so we may begin practicing our Mediumship.

The stationary person thus becomes a *"Medium"* or *"Reader"*, and the person setting their chair down in front of us becomes the *"Sitter"*.

Immediately a stranger, who just positioned a chair in front of mine, is staring and smiling. He is tall, has a blonde ponytail and is wearing a leather jacket. I had seen him earlier in the day, when he was talking with a group of people before class. At that time, I assumed he was an accomplished Medium – and that this wasn't his "first rodeo".

Here he is... sitting... smiling... extending his hand in greeting.

Cheryn Ryan

He shakes my hand and tells me his name is Beau.

I think I'm going to be sick at my stomach as I consider running from this room, while loudly screaming,

"I'm a FAKE... I don't know what to do... I can't do this... I shouldn't be here... I'm sorry!"

I tell him this is my first time to attempt a reading for someone. He smiles knowingly and says,

"Don't worry, I understand. We've all been beginners, at some point."

This declaration does nothing to alleviate my fears.

Although I had just done a successful psychic reading, which I was fairly sure was the extent of my spiritual gifts and didn't include mediumship, I begin my reading.

We are holding hands, as I say a short prayer. I ask for guidance and clarity and the best way to bring messages of love for this

The Surprised Medium

man. I also find myself asking Spirit, to not make me look like a total loser.

Uh-Oh! ... I think I'm freaking out!

He expects me to say something ... something profound! This man expects me to give him "Heavenly Messages"!

"Where is the door?"

"How fast can I gather my handbag and sweater?"

"I can pretend to be ill and just leave!"

"THAT'S IT! ... I'll leave without saying a word! I can do this ..."

What???

"That" voice ... is talking to me...

That voice which has, in the past, told me,

"Act now! ... "Move into another lane!" ... "Don't go to that party tonight." ... "No worry, everything is ok!"

Yeah ... **THAT Voice** ... is saying,

"Say Ray!"

I say,

"Ray".

(No words from this stranger sitting here. No blink, no wink, no squirming in his seat -- *NO NOTHING!*)

The Voice says,

The Surprised Medium

"*Say Ray ... <u>Again</u>!*"

And I say,

"*I'm supposed to say Ray, again.*"

And, again, *nothing* from Beau. No reaction. No words. (I assume I'm making this up, but I keep going, because that is the assignment, and I did hear *"that"* voice.)

As I wait silently for some reaction, I plainly see a memory in my mind's eye; I see a vision of my grandmother, my own sweet grandmother, Anna Lee. She is peeling apples and handing them to me and I feel the overwhelming love she has for me. I see and I feel the love that radiated between her and me and I mention that love to Beau.

Then I see another woman, a mother figure step forward and I know ... *I just KNOW*, this is Beau's mom! She is standing next to him and telling me she loves him so much.

I say,

Cheryn Ryan

"I believe you and your grandmother had a special bond. She loves you very much. She was quite a force in your life! She was really close to you and your mother, who is here, also. Your mother tells me she loves you so very, very much. She and your grandmother are both extremely proud of you."

This is incredible to me, *because I actually feel the love* this man's mother and grandmother have for him!

Next, I see two male figures bringing forth love for this stranger who is still sitting silently in front of me.

I say,

"There is a tall man, who reminds me of Abraham Lincoln, and he's standing on a fishing pier with a rod and reel. I believe this man was a father-figure to you and was instrumental in raising you. He's very proud of you, too."

The Surprised Medium

"Abe" disappears and another tall man comes into my mind, and he tells me he is Beau's father.

"Your dad just arrived. He says he is very sorry for not being in your life. He says he is ashamed of his actions, leaving you and your mother. He knows it was hard for you and your mother, and he now understands how his leaving impacted your life."

He is telling me,

"You stood the test of time, you stayed the course! You persevered and became a wonderful man. I'm so very proud of you. Please forgive me, I love you."

(A bell is ringing to mark the end of our session.)

I look at Beau. He has tears streaming down his face.

I wait, silently, as he begins telling me how accurate my reading has been.

Cheryn Ryan

"Raelene was my grandmother, everyone called her "Rae"; I was her world, we were very close, and I miss her so much! My Mom and I lived with my grandmother because my father left us. Mom was a great mother to me."

"Raymond was my uncle, my "Uncle Ray". He took the place of my dad in my life. He taught me so much! He loved to fish and taught me how, and so many other things in life. He was tall and he actually looked a bit like Abraham Lincoln."

My mouth is wide open, I'm totally flabbergasted! I have just been privileged to see and feel the intense love and emotion from several strangers -- one sitting right in front of me, and four in Heaven!

Beau's family simply trusted me with their messages for him, and I shared them with their loving child. I had no idea the impact this would have, until I saw his tears ... and felt mine, filling my eyes and running down my face.

The Surprised Medium

I wiped my cheeks, as Beau told me this,

"Cheryn, you just connected with my family, and I'm so very, very thankful! My dad, saying he was sorry, means a lot to me -- as does **everything** you've said in the last few minutes. Thank you so very much! You definitely have a wonderful gift!"

What an experience! *What a life-changing experience!* I recognized this exchange as the start of my journey as a Medium.

I whisper to myself,

"Hello Worlds! I want to be of service."

Cheryn Ryan

Before "Say Ray!"

I come from a line of strong, incredible women -- My mother, my grandmothers, my undiscovered many Great-Great Grandmothers. I believe the majority of my innate instincts and gifts came down from them.

I look at actual photos from my life and I see whispers of light surrounding some of the people in those pictures. I have two photos of my grandmother and me, encircled by Spirit Light, which leads me to believe my Mediumship is an inherited gift.

.

I see that light in my granddaughter's photograph, when I gave her her aunt's doll collection; I can almost see my daughter, Christy beside her! The first photo taken of Carl and me was months after Christy passed and she's very evident in that one. How that works? I don't know! I just know these precious pictures of my life reflect Spirit

The Surprised Medium

People "hanging around", and that brings me comfort.

My mother, Christine, worked as a Purchasing Agent for a large petrochemical company on the Houston Ship Channel. In addition to putting in twenty-five years there, she raised four children – three somewhat "normal" kids, and me -- a Psychic and Medium.

Mom was beautiful. Her hair was always styled and she was able to dress stylishly, even on our strict family budget. People who didn't know her intimately, didn't know what a big heart she had. She was a woman who quietly reached out and helped people in trouble. When her friends complained of an ailment, she gave them massages. She counseled neighborhood women who were suffering from family problems. She prepared cakes and casseroles for neighbors, co-workers, and friends experiencing health issues or loss of loved ones. She regularly sent note cards to people who needed a little loving attention. She gave them hope for tomorrow.

Mom was the youngest child in her family. When she was seven years old, her only brother, Shirley died. Shirley was an Eagle Scout, a Scout leader, and company apprentice when he passed suddenly of Juvenile Diabetes. Her other siblings, older sisters were married and out on their own, so young Christine took on the task of trying to raise the spirits of people in her life.

My grandparents were devastated, of course, and my sweet mother decided to entertain them, everyway a young child could. She created plays and performances, and insisted her parents participate in the productions. She invited friends and family to join in, too. Neighbors, church members, and family were invited to be involved and to help with the task of creating joy, where none existed.

The Surprised Medium

The practice of creating happy diversions, fun parties and elaborate celebrations for others stayed with my mother all her life. I grew up enjoying every holiday gathering Mom supervised with love.

I Thank God for All my Blessings

Cheryn Ryan

Growing up, I saw Mom plan our family's next gathering, *as we were enjoying each current one*! Mom loved having her brood around; she loved entertaining us. She relished our talks, storytelling and laughter during our dinners and knock-it-out-of-the-park family card games. Both my parents were intimidating opponents; I can still hear Mom shouting *"Skip-Bo!"* now.

Mom studied astrology and appreciated natural healing remedies. She practiced massage therapy, which she learned from her oldest sister, Irene. Irene was a very good business woman; She was President of one of Ohio's Real Estate Organizations and owned a trendy spa for women in Akron, Ohio, where Mom was a willing guinea pig. Mom had a strong belief in Christianity, God, and Heaven and she and Dad were loving, caring people and excellent parents.

Mom and I never talked about visits from loved ones who had passed, but she did tell

The Surprised Medium

me once, both she and my grandmother, Anna Lee, had prophetic dreams that came true. After I discovered I had psychic instincts and shared them with Dad and Mom, Mom told me these *"ran in our family"*. I realized her big brother, my Uncle Shirley, must have visited with her regularly to help her and her family cope with his early death.

One day when we were talking about vivid dreams, Mom told me about one she had had. As a young married woman with a soldier husband, she shared how she had worried and waited for Dad to return home after WWII.

Millions of people around the world awaited their loved ones' return. Soldiers were coming back to the U.S. in droves and Mom was concerned about Dad's delayed homecoming from Europe. She grew anxious and one day asked her mother,

"Mama, have a dream, and tell me when Cliff will be back".

Cheryn Ryan

My grandmother answered,

"Have your own dream, My Child."

... And, SHE DID!

My mother went to sleep that same night and had a crystal-clear dream. In her dream, she was wearing her wedding gown, and standing alone in the front of the church where she and Dad had been married, four and a half years before. As she waited, at the altar, Dad opened the church doors and walked down the aisle toward her. Six months later, Dad arrived home at 11:55 p.m. -- on their fifth wedding anniversary!

Cliff and Chris Ryan, 1945

MY PSYCHIC CHILDHOOD

I grew up in a loving and very busy household. All my friends were close to my age. There were so many of us! I thought all the world was one happy place, filled with friends just like mine. We had a care-free existence, playing hopscotch, Red Rover, baseball, hide 'n seek and staying out after dark, to capture fireflies in the summer time.

I loved Lucy and Ricky and all the simple sweet shows on TV. I loved my family. I loved my school and my friends. I loved the swimming pool down the street. And I loved my red and yellow bike -- that "Christmas Morning Bicycle", which my parents bought from a neighbor and re-painted to make appear "new". I love my parents, both in Heaven.

My mom went to work in an office when my brother, the youngest child in our family, started public school. Dad was a manufacturer's representative and worked primarily from home, so there was usually an adult around. We lived in a nice neighborhood, where I *"knew"* the stories within the walls of almost all eighty homes!

My Life is Full of Peace, Love, Laughter, and Light

I was a curious kid, I wanted to know how things worked, how people lived, how the earth moved, how and why people we love, leave. I was curious about how my Mamaw survived after my Papaw died. I was curious about Anne Frank, about where her spirit went when she died. I wondered if there really was a fire-filled place called Hell. I wondered what happened to Hitler after he died. I wanted to know *"Everything"*!

I recall often lying in the cool grass of our lawn and looking up at the clouds during the day and the stars at night, and thinking,

The Surprised Medium

"This isn't all there is to life …There's a lot more they're not telling me, and I want to know what it is!"

There is a feeling of sadness that has appeared often in my life. I now know it is because I'm an Empath – that is, I feel other people's emotions, which is the main reason why I *"know things"* about people. Although I have been befuddled by it, this ability has served me well through the years, and I am grateful.

I felt and heard things about people in my life. I knew if a schoolmate, neighbor or friend was despondent, or in trouble of some sort, however I didn't understand that feeling. If church or neighborhood adults had problems, I knew something was askew; I just didn't know what or why.

Cheryn Ryan

Cheryn, age 12 with Anna Lee Huff, her grandmother, and Spirit Light

I believed a perfect world existed everywhere, until I read books about the Holocaust and the atomic bombs that were dropped on Japan. Then I was over-whelmed with such a deep sadness, the kind which so many people have experienced in their lifetimes.

I had feelings that ran the gambit from good to bad, normal to weird. Mr. C bothered me. Mrs. P bothered me. Both Mr. and Mrs. D bothered me. (*"Bothered"* is a relative term, perhaps *"worried"* is a better word to describe my feelings.) I felt and knew things before actually hearing my parents or other adults mention something about them. (By the way, my hearing is acute, always has been, and I probably heard more than I should have at a tender age.) I liked to hang out with adults back then; Their inner most thoughts were intriguing, to a young psychic!

My own religious up-bringing was lovely, but it lacked information I found wanting. I follow Christ's teachings and I believe we all go to what I still call "Heaven", where we are tasked with learning more about eternal life, being of service to others, loving all people, animals, and our world. I believe we all strive to reach goals set by our own soul and by

Cheryn Ryan

Great Holy Spirit, in order to evolve; We all wish to evolve to become more perfect souls.

I Awake for a Joyful Day

One of my gifts which most likely connects to Mediumship, is when I absolutely knew if someone was nice or not. I always thought it was me simply making up "stories" about people I did not, or barely, knew. I did this with strangers passing by. I sat in the back seat of our family car, and when a car passed, I *"made up a story"* to go along with the people in that car -- At least, I thought I was making up stories! As it turned out, I wasn't.

A man and woman, who lived down the street from my family, had a young son who died. Every time I walked passed their home, I felt sadness all around. A year or two later, they adopted a little boy and their home seemed happy again. I was so thrilled for them!

The Surprised Medium

I later discovered some of my thoughts weren't "mine". They were messages from Spirit -- my Guardian Angels and my Heavenly Guides -- giving me information to either help others, to help keep me safe, or to learn something important from them.

If I was around people who made me uncomfortable, I absolutely knew they were not trustworthy and I decided to stay away from them. I recall having a neighbor a few blocks away whom we didn't know well, and we later learned was a criminal. I couldn't stand the sight of him!

Did my siblings know such things? Not that they told me. I know my brother did have an out of body experience and my older sister is often reminded of her loved ones through different encounters, like hearing a familiar song.

My very first recollection of what was to come was when I was eight years old and had my tonsils removed. On the way to the

Cheryn Ryan

hospital, Mom asked me if I had any questions.

Of course, I did! I had received that glorious red and yellow bicycle for Christmas, just a few months prior and I had a sneaking suspicion Dad had painted it, himself.

"Mom, is Santa Claus real?"

She smiled at my question and told me the who, how, and why of Christmas! (I happily clarified any "misunderstanding" my younger sister held about Santa a few weeks later.)

After Mom and I checked in at the hospital's admitting office, a nurse who spoke in an accent foreign to my eight-year-old ears, placed a mask over my mouth and nose. I went down a swirling, long tunnel. I was terribly scared. When I woke, I remember thinking I had died, but nothing else. I now think I had a near-death experience. Thankfully, I returned and continued to live a nice life in suburbia.

The Surprised Medium

Rick

Rick was the only son of my parents' dear friends, Dick and Ellie. He was my age and we met only three or four times, but I felt a connection during our long-distant vacations to visit with their family.

His family lived in the Frozen North and ours, in the Hot South. When I was around 20 years old, I read one of Ellie's letter to Mom. In her letter, she mentioned Rick had completed his training and had become an airplane pilot. I knew in that very moment, Rick would die in a plane crash -- actually, I didn't *know*, I had a very strong feeling that is how his life would end.

Although we weren't in touch and I was probably just a vague memory of his, I thought about him a lot. Every time, after the premonition of his death came to me, I checked the names of the pilot and co-pilot whenever I flew. I'm certain I would have turned around and found an alternate flight, if Rick was the pilot on board. I certainly would have warned him, even though I didn't yet have the words and knowledge to explain my belief. I wished I had warned him, regardless.

Rick died when his airplane crashed.

The Surprised Medium

Tea

My next experience – another very vivid experience - was when my mom's best friend, Tea Johnson McHugh, came to visit me in my dreams.

My mom and dad had plane reservations and plans to leave in two weeks to go abroad and visit with Tea and her nephew in Australia. It had been over a decade since they and Tea were together, and they were looking so forward to being with them.

In my dream, Tea was standing tall and lovely, and was next to my grandmother, Anna Lee. I knew, without a doubt, Tea had died, because my grandmother had died twenty years before.

Cheryn Ryan

Cheryn, age 15 with her grandmother, Anna Lee Huff, and Spirit Light

I drove to my parents' home the next morning to tell them what had happened. Mom and Dad trusted what I told them,

The Surprised Medium

and were obviously extremely saddened by this news.

Bernie, Tea's nephew called later that day to confirm what we already knew. I had always felt close to Tea, and I suppose coming to me, and through me, was the best way to soften the news of her passing to her loving friends.

Cheryn Ryan

Mick

One day, while dating my former husband, we were at a restaurant, discussing many topics. He stopped abruptly and told me he had a "very special gift" for me.

At that very moment, I thought,

"I have too many purses, I don't need another one, what in the world is he thinking?"

He changed the subject and I soon forgot about the purse, until a month later, when he gave me a lovely hand-tooled leather handbag he had made.

Another interesting incidence, happened one Christmas, after we had married. My husband handed me a small package. *Immediately* I knew it was an address book.

The Surprised Medium

He noticed *"that look"* on my face and asked me what I thought it was. I replied,

"It's an address book."

He looked shocked and said,

"Ok, Miss Smarty Pants, what's in in it?"

I answered,

"Money."

I opened the wrapping paper to discover *my* old address book, which held a massage therapist's name, phone number and $50! *(Yay!)*

I was almost certain, at that point in time, I could "read minds" and was somewhat thrilled; My husband was quite upset.

After those experiences, and seeing my husband's obvious fear, I questioned my spiritual path. When "odd" things occurred, I accepted them in virtual silence.

Cheryn Ryan

Don

One of my life's dearest gifts was given to me by Don, who was married to my mother-in-law. I had been told about his questionable past and I felt negative vibrations around when we were together. He often challenged me to trivia from the Bible when we saw each other, as if he was trying to prove how "saintly" or "religious" he was.

Don had a heart attack and was in a hospital ICU for thirteen days. His doctors did not expect him to recover, yet he made it out of there and into a private room. We were called late that night and my husband, his mother, and I went to the hospital to check on Don.

The Surprised Medium

Mick and his mother left immediately to go outside for a smoke, and I was alone with this man, who didn't like me very much.

As I poured him some water, covered him with an extra blanket, and asked if he wanted to talk about *anything* --

Don sat straight up in his bed and said,

"YES! ... That woman, from the Dominican Republic, who was in the bed next to me, died and All Her People came! ... It was the most incredible thing I've ever seen! ... There were colors -- like nothing here ... and flowers -- I've never seen before! ... It was the most beautiful thing! ... I can't even describe it! Colors you wouldn't believe, flowers, unlike our flowers here ... everywhere! And Everyone was Happy, and Joyful, and Laughing, and It was Beautiful, It was Wonderful!"

I told him I believed we are greeted by our loved ones immediately upon leaving our bodies and I asked him,

"After everything you've been through, are you afraid to die?"

He responded,

"No! … But I'm NOT going <u>that way</u>, I'm going in the Way of the Lord … not like her!"

I thought to myself,

"<u>That</u> is the Way we ALL go, Don, and You were just shown a wonderful preview… You were shown A little slice of Heaven!"

Life Goes On

(Fast forward a couple of years . . .)

After Aunt Tea died, and Don recovered, I continued to have dreams, premonitions, and very strong beliefs, which I mostly kept to myself.

Instead of reading every-day novels, I read, and read, and read about encounters of every-day people who had connections with their loved ones in Heaven.

My days were really busy raising my children and trying to maintain that doomed marriage. Doomed? Yes. Mick was scared of my ability -- not really scared of things that Holy Spirit gave me, but worried that I *knew* about *his* extra-curricular life. *I did.* I absolutely knew every time he lied, every time he was out on the town without his wife and children.

A couple of examples, which showed his utter contempt for my gift, happened one summer, when we were on vacation. As we were approaching our campsite, from a night out, I told him we had a "notice of some-sort, on the front door of our R.V." and asked him to keep the engine running.

He reacted by saying,

"What the Hell?"

I got out of our pick-up truck and went to retrieve the note, the note I *knew* was there. The message on our door was from the camp manager, stating our house sitter asked us to call him. I *felt* everything was ok, because Spirit had told me, as I called our friend and discovered our car was missing from our driveway. It took me a minute but, I realized my father had borrowed it and had failed to tell our house sitter!

Allow my Voice to Speak Your Truth

The Surprised Medium

Another time, on that same vacation, I said to my husband,

"We better stop and adjust the bikes." Referring to bicycles strapped between our pick up truck and our rented R.V.

He shouted, angrily,

"Do you mind if I wait until I find a better place to pull over?"

Two minutes later, the bikes came untied and crashed, causing seven hundred dollars worth of damage. Boy, was he upset after that!

I'm definitely certain, someone who discovers they are married to a Psychic Medium might be scared, if they're a non-believer, but he *knew* me -- knew me as a Christian, a good person, a good wife, and mother.

Cheryn Ryan

My knowledge about his dis-functional family and abusive childhood gave me compassion for his path in life. I understood his fears and tried my very best to help him overcome them. In the end, he refused to be a loving partner and eventually our marriage ended.

The Surprised Medium

Pat

One July night, my friend, Pat, took her own life. It was the night of my high school reunion.

My husband and I had gotten to bed around two o'clock and I fell into a deep sleep as soon as my head hit the pillow. I dreamed Pat was seriously ill and she needed immediate help. My husband was with me in the dream, and I told him we needed to knock down a door to reach her. He kicked it through and we entered her room. Even though Pat was almost as tall as I in "real" life, in this dream I easily scooped her up and ran to our car. My husband drove like a race car driver to the hospital. We went dangerously up and down esplanades, around sharp corners, through crowds of cars and people. We finally arrived and I got out of the car and carried Pat toward the Emergency Room. As I walked to the entrance, the door swung open and a nurse came toward me and declared,

"I'm sorry, she's dead."

I woke, in tears, and could not go back to sleep. I didn't understand my bizarre dream. I considered the evening out, the reunion, seeing old friends, etc. I questioned myself until I justified the nightmare and blamed it on food and drink, but I lay awake for hours. When I finally fell back to sleep, my phone rang – it was one of our friends, telling me Pat had died.

In the end, Pat didn't want to kill herself; She wanted to live. How do I know this? She told me in my sleep ... separated by 17 miles. Not on the phone, or in a letter. She told me in *that* dream. *She wanted help, she wanted to be saved,* however I didn't recognize the urgency for quick action, and for notifying her family. No one was able to act in time to save her.

The Surprised Medium

Pat was a good person who loved her daughter and sons. She was loving and giving and energetic – full of fun and mischief and she had a deep longing to be loved by her unaffectionate mother. She was continuously searching for happiness; Though she had glimpses of it, she was inwardly very sad.

It is my very strong belief, as Pat began to end her life that night, she realized that was not the way for her to die, and she struggled to come back. I so wish I had known then, what I know now. Perhaps my help would have made a difference, perhaps not. I know one thing, her passing made a significant difference in my life.

What did I do next? I went on living a simple life in Suburbia, because I had children to raise, a home to overlook and an increasingly angry husband to placate.

Then, my young friend, Jo died.

Ever-lasting Life Does Exist

Cheryn Ryan

Jo

Jo was my 25 year old friend. She was vivacious, intelligent, and a kind young woman. She was an active business woman who loved sports and sailing. One day, she showed me some weird spots appearing on her body and said she planned a doctor's visit that week. I had an overwhelming feeling she was seriously ill. When she went, her physicians discovered she had advanced cancer that had metastasized.

I was on vacation in another country when Jo died. I was so upset that such a fine young woman, my friend had left. I was totally overcome with sadness. I was sad that such a young, vital woman died prematurely, sad that I had missed her memorial service, and sad that I didn't have the opportunity to give her one last hug good-bye.

The Surprised Medium

Two weeks passed and I had another incredible dream.

Jo sat directly across a table from me. She was *really* there! She looked radiant. I had seen her hair in a ponytail -- never in another style, yet in this meeting she wore her blond hair down, across her shoulders and she was wearing a lovely white dress. She was smiling, brilliantly, and she looked at me and said,

"Everything's Ok, don't worry anymore. I'm fine!"

I woke up crying, yet feeling very loved.

These two dreams -- from my friends, Pat and Jo -- meant so very, very much to me! *Two of my friends had reached through time and space to communicate with me!*

The difference in this dream, and the one with Pat, is I *KNEW* instantly this was Jo, and I *KNEW -- Without a Doubt,* she was still alive!

After my visit with Jo, I decided to use every avenue I could to seek information to help explain the things I had experienced. I

Cheryn Ryan

started exploring real-life stories of other people who had reached through that veil between this life and our next life.

The Surprised Medium

Cheryn

And,

Mediums Grieve, Too

My darling oldest child, my daughter, Christy, died at the age of 30 and I grieve her early passing ... *every single moment.*

Our beloved Christy is still in my life, in some way, day in and day out. I miss her human presence, I miss her smile, her laughter, her style, her observations about life, her kindness and the loving way she treated everyone. I miss everything about her, AND I know she is on her own new life's path and she is still helping me and others on ours.

I cannot gloss over the fact that my child died. Everyone has heard:

Cheryn Ryan

"Losing a child is the most horrific thing that can happen to a loving parent."

and I can attest to that. Many times after she passed I wanted to die, but I kept trudging on because *I know she is ok*, and has joined Great Holy Spirit.

I Am Thankful for Everyday Miracles

The Surprised Medium

My sweet girl sends me messages that I call *"small miracles"* almost daily, and I'm always thrilled! Every time, I thank her for her continued love.

At this time in my life, I have received thousands of notifications from her on-going life. They sometimes come in droves, sometimes in dribbles, often in huge waves; And, more often than not, in surprising ways.

Here are a few of the more outstanding notifications I've received from her:

Cheryn Ryan

My radio turns on – *by "itself"* -- and plays really significant songs – songs that Christy loved, and are so special to both of us ...

"Unchained Melody"..."You and Me Against the World" ... "My Girl"... "When You Wish Upon a Star" have all mysteriously turned on -- with no prompting or button pushing from me or another human.

I see lights flashing *on and off*, and I've observed them at my church, while shopping, and in my home. Mostly, they alert me to look at an object that is significant to Christy and me. Different lights, at different times just start blinking and then stop. It is a treat, a little gift for me, from my sweet girl.

Small gifts present themselves, as if unattached to anything else, *except* I do have the recognition that these little miracles are being sent by Spirit and by my daughter.

When my precious daughter, Christy, died and my heart was breaking, a white butterfly landed right in the middle of my chest and

The Surprised Medium

stayed there for over thirty minutes, as I was walking and crying in the woods.

A week after she passed on July 4th, I heard *Christy's voice*, and I saw a signal flare in the middle of the Houston Ship Channel. Apparently, no one else observed it, or notified authorities. Perhaps people simply passed it off, as many partiers were still celebrating our American Independence with fireworks. However, I *knew* exactly what I saw, because Christy told me,

"*Look, Mom!*"

Christy had been an avid swimmer and scuba diver, in addition to her hiking, playing softball, kick-boxing and volleyball. As a teen she was a volunteer turtle egg conservator, when we lived in the Virgin Islands. She was one of the most compassionate people I knew, and I know, *without a doubt*, Christy would have gone out in a boat herself to save people in trouble.

Cheryn Ryan

So, I called the Coast Guard. At first, the Officer on Duty was un-convinced and thought I might have seen fireworks, instead of a distress flare. I told him I was *certain* of the situation and that young man and I worked together to triangulate and determine the exact spot the flare originated.

The officer sent a rescue helicopter, which twenty minutes later discovered a pleasure boat adrift; It was a 40 foot boat, without lights, without power, in the dark, and in eminent danger in the shipping lane of one of the busiest ports in the United States!

I am totally convinced, Christy and the Coast Guard helped save seventeen people's lives that night!

Every year, on Christy's birthday, I celebrate her Earth life. I go out to eat Mexican or Thai food for lunch, next I go to a movie she would have liked and/or I search for a special gift for us at a consignment or re-sale shop. We both love re-sale stores, and the mystery and excitement of finding a treasure!

The Surprised Medium

One year, I had exactly $1.43 in change in my purse. I stopped at a shop in Kyle, Texas and found a very old, home-made, stitched fabric sign that read:

"One Hand, One Heart."

The significance? Christy and I both collected ceramic hands (she gave me some of the ones I have), and that precious little framed art piece was for sale for *"Cash Only, $1.25"!*

Last year, Christy sent me some earrings through my friend, Jane, who was clearing out jewelry she no longer wore. Unbeknown to Jane, the earrings she gave me were of a design and style Christy really liked. When I turned them over, I laughed and cried. The name stamped on the back of both earrings is "Otto" – the name Christy always used as her name for reservations and passwords -- AND the name of her beloved cat, Otto!

This year on Christy's birthday, I needed a small box to house some inspirational cards I own. I decided to ask her help to find the "perfect box", birthday gift for us.

I walked into a Goodwill store, and without hesitation, was told: *"Turn Right"*; I immediately turned right, then I was told to *"Turn at Your Next Left"*; I did, and I looked on the shelf directly in front of me -- there sat the *perfect little box* with these words,

"Mother, the One who bears the Sweetest Name"!

Ah, my beautiful daughter showered me with her love again!

Early on, about nine months after her passing, Christy gave me one of the most unusual and wonderful gifts in this world.

I was resolved to visit a Medium that a co-worker had told me about. The thing that attracted me to this particular Medium, was the fact her reputation for honesty was extremely high *and* she lived four hours away from me, and would not have access to my

The Surprised Medium

personal information. (I really should not have worried about that!)

I was skeptical, so I called her from another friend's phone; I did not give my last name; I did not tell her anything about me; She did not know I was calling from a distant city. I made an appointment for the following week.

My visit to Linda Drake was actually my first visit to a Medium. I was ready to pounce and challenge her and to declare her reading "not actual enough". I was totally caught off-guard when I walked into Linda's home and she greeted me with,

"Hello Cheryn! It's so nice to meet you. You're here to meet with your daughter, she's right behind you."

Cheryn Ryan

(From <u>Reaching Through the Veil to Heal</u> by Linda Drake)

I had heard of Linda through a woman who worked for the same company that I did. This woman and I worked independently at our own homes, and I had met her only once and felt immediately that we had a connection. On the phone, we shared memories about our daughters, who both had died, and shared feelings about the difficulty of living without them. She called one day to give me a telephone number that had been passed on to her by her friend in

The Surprised Medium

Austin. She told me about Linda and her ability to connect people with their loved ones who had died. I called Linda and made an appointment, giving her just my name. When I showed up for the appointment, Linda greeted me, we walked into her office, and she said, "You're here to meet with your daughter. She's right behind you."

From there our session continued with Linda validating many, many things for me. She talked about instances in my daughter's life that she could not have known without help from God and my daughter. I broke down when Linda said she was unwrapping candy – butterscotch candy. My dad had always greeted Christy with a little piece of butterscotch candy from his pocket. Linda talked about milestones in my daughter's life and I came to the conclusion that Linda has a divine gift to help those of us here to carry on, until we cross over and join our loved ones. I had experienced visits from Christy before I met Linda, but that visit was the step I needed on my road to recovery. I am convinced our spirit does live on and that our transition into the next place is just that – a transition. I now understand and accept the grace of God.

My mouth must have fallen open, and stayed that way all through the very specific reading Linda gave me. I was bowled over, when she clearly explained so many things -- things, only I knew.

I have been glad to recommend Linda Drake to others seeking solace in their lives. Linda is the real deal.

Linda and I share a close mutual friend, Phyllis. One day, a couple of years later, that dear friend, Phyllis was parked outside in her car, waiting for me to finish my session with Linda, so we could all go to lunch nearby -- when she received the following text message from my daughter, on *her* cell phone.

This was a number of years ago and I had never -- ever, even seen a "text" before that day!

Here is that message:

The Surprised Medium

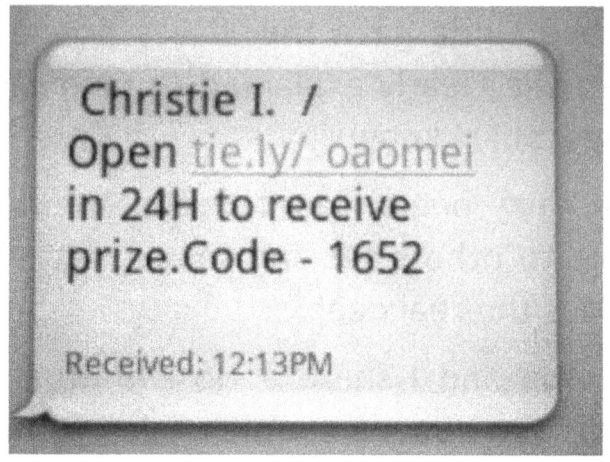

My daughter's name: **Christy Lynn**,

Her birthday is the **24th**

Christy's *only niece and nephew – <u>who were not yet born</u>* ... Have birthdays on the

12th and the 13th *Those were the <u>future birthdays</u> of my son's daughter (the 13th) and his son (the 12th)

Christy's "Text Present" appeared to say:

"I love you, Mommy (tie.ly/oaomei) -- and I'm still around!"

Cheryn Ryan

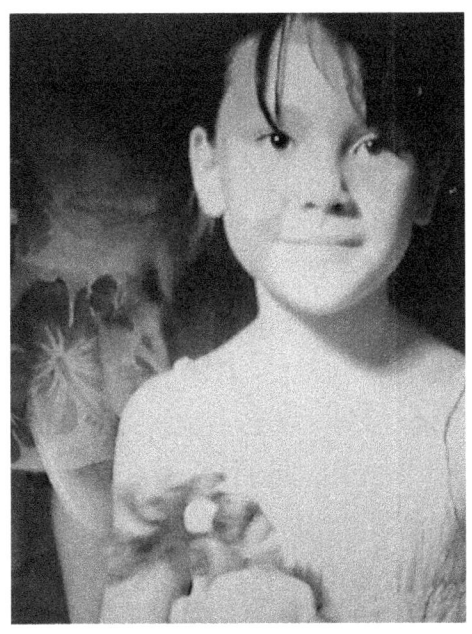

My Granddaughter Karuna, holding her aunt Christy's doll. Christy appears to be smiling at Karuna's right shoulder.

Again, I had never seen a text; I didn't even know what they were! Phyllis had only received a few simple texts from her workplace and family, prior to this. I took a photo and saved it to share with others. It is my most prized possession.

The Surprised Medium

About Phyllis -- she recently passed and my heart was torn, as we were life-long friends and committed believers in Our Awesome God. I was lost for a while, missing her so!

I expected her to appear to me soon after her passing, but she didn't, and I was really upset! Four months later, just after another of our childhood friends had passed, she brought Harry (that school friend -- our teen year's *"heartthrob"* and undoubtedly, one of the *most* handsome boys we knew back in the day) to simply say *"Hi!"* to me. He gave me a kiss on my cheek, as Phyllis grinned in the background. Then, we all had a good laugh.

The things Phyllis and I shared – the laughter, fun times, poignant stories, and our devout belief that life continues after our body dies, makes me very thankful for our life-long friendship. I know she'll be one of the Souls that greet me as I pass from this life.

Cheryn Ryan

Miracles occur Everywhere, Every Day!

Inanimate objects fly; Lights blink on and off; Music plays by itself; Special mementos appear, as if by magic; People reach out, unexpectedly to share stories about our loved ones; Loving voices are heard and visions are seen; Special memories, songs, and scents fill our senses with joy, if we allow them to!

The Surprised Medium

Michelle

Michelle, my "heart daughter", believes in God and Holy Spirit and the numerous accounts of loving visitations that have shown up in her life.

Michelle and I were standing in my kitchen one day and talking about her cousin, Spring's recent wedding, which she had attended. Immediately, I saw their deceased grandmother, wearing a 1950's style hat, and told Michelle,

Lovely, articulate, intelligent Michelle, my heart daughter

"Your grandmother was there, and I believe Spring wore a vintage dress and hat, am I right?"

Michelle smiled and said,

"Yes, she wore one of Grandmother's hats!"

And ... at that very moment, water started flowing -- by "itself", from my kitchen faucet, three feet away from both of us!

Michelle and I both cracked up at this incredible show of presence from her loving grandmother -- which has never happened to me, before or again!

The Surprised Medium

Ryan

My son, Ryan, who grew up with my sharing spiritual thoughts and beliefs, often accompanied me to church, and graduated from a Presbyterian Church Affiliated College.

Ryan, my funny, smart, and charismatic son

Cheryn Ryan

He now points out --

"Don't call other people weird, Mom … YOU are the WEIRD one!"

Ryan believes in our continuing adventures after this life, yet still holds a healthy skepticism about it. The following cannot be denied, however, and he feels the love that permeated this happening.

My husband, children Christy and Ryan, and I moved to the Caribbean when my children were young. Our family became friends with a number of other families, one of which, consisted of a mother, father and two sons. One of those sons, Andy was a year older than my son. Soon after their initial meeting, Andy and Ryan became inseparable as elementary school classmates and best friends on St. Croix.

When they were in the first and second grades, I drove them, along with two other school mates, to the far side of the island … in the middle of the night, to see Halley's Comet in the south-eastern sky. That night, those four boys decided to meet the next time the comet came close to Earth -- in seventy-five years. It was a promise they all expected to keep.

Time went by, and my husband and I moved our family back to Texas. Before we returned to the states, Andy created and presented to Ryan, a lovely photo album full of pictures and notes about the times they shared together. It was a treasured gift to a boy leaving his best friend.

Fast forward to Ryan's first year of college and his desire to meet up with Andy again. Ryan called his phone number in St. Croix and was told the story of Andy's recent passing.

Andy was an active, fun-loving young man and he was always trying new and daring adventures. On the last occasion, he had been free diving in the ocean, lost consciousness and drowned.

Cheryn Ryan

Ryan and I were devastated. This was his second close friend who died quite young and Ryan took this news very hard.

Fast Forward, Seven More Years ...

Ryan was living in Hawaii and called me at home in Texas one morning to chat, and to let me know he was going to hitchhike across the island to apply for a second part-time job. He assured me it was a safe way to travel on island and said he'd send me an email to let me know how the interview went.

I was totally surprised to get another call from him later that day, because his phone calls home had been few and far between.

He proceeded to recall his latest adventure,

"Mom, you're not going to believe what happened! When I finished the interview, I walked for a bit and was picked up by a man diving in my direction. He had three other guys in tow, too. I got in the car and introduced myself to the crowd. Someone asked me

where I was from, and I told them *Texas and St. Croix.*"

"One of the guys looked shocked and said,

"Did you know Andy?"

I replied,

"Andy was my best friend."

The other guy was clearly surprised and responded,

"Andy was my best friend, too!"

These two young men -- Each, who shared a deep affection for Andy, met ... on the *other side of the world ... on an island ... while one of them was hitchhiking!*

They commiserated about their great friend and how he had affected their lives in similar ways, and about <u>how he had arranged their meeting right then and there</u>!

When Ryan returned home, he called Andy's parents and shared this wonderful encounter with them. Andy had worked very hard -- *or what we humans imagine as hard --* to bring his two dear friends close.

That "Hawaiian Meet-Up" was planned a long time in advance of that day!

Andy worked to orchestrate the following:

To have the driver decide to go that long distance, on that particular day.

To make Andy's other friend ride along.

To tell Ryan about the job opening, beforehand.

To manipulate Ryan's schedule going and returning to allow him to be in the exact spot ... at the exact time ... the car was passing by.

To make the driver stop and pick up Ryan, even though his car was full.

This is a Miracle

This is Serendipity

This is Heaven Talking to Us

The Surprised Medium

Ben, Christy, and David

Ben is my nephew. He's kind and smart and fun to be with, and he works at the Texas Medical Center Library, in Houston.

One night after work, he called for an Uber. When the driver, David picked him up, the two men shared small talk on the ride home.

David told Ben he had worked, years before, at Baylor College of Medicine. Ben mentioned his mother, Mona, and other members of our family who had been employed there, as well. David said,

Cheryn Ryan

"Ben, I knew your mom and your cousin, Christy, too!"

On the drive home, they talked about Christy and the fact David had attended her memorial service, but had to leave, as it was too emotional for him.

He said he had always wanted to contact Christy's mom to share his condolences, but he had failed to do so. Ben called me the next day and told me about meeting up with David. I called David, and as a result, we have become friends as we share loving stories about my wonderful daughter -- David's dear friend.

You Are a Cherished Child of God

Christy cared for so many people, and David is one of them. I'm so thankful millions of us know that connection between our Earthly life and Heaven is only a thought away.

The Surprised Medium

Something happened another time, pertaining to Christy's work at the Medical Center. It was only five months after Christy passed and my sister-in-law's birthday sneaked up on me. I was visiting my sister, and she had forgotten Mona's birthday, too. She searched in her desk for an appropriate birthday card and pulled out a small box with greeting cards inside and said,

"This will do for a birthday card, right?"

I gasped and asked her where she had gotten the cards. She looked quizzically at me and replied she had bought them at a neighbor's yard sale. I recognized these cards as ones my Christy had hand decorated and given out to friends and co-workers for Christmas gifts!

She investigated and found the young woman, Val had worked with Christy. She told us Christy was one of the kindest people she had ever encountered, and that Christy was always preparing special dishes and treats for her co-workers. Val told us Christy had made the cards for Christmas gifts last year. I recognized them because Christy had also given me one of the cards for my birthday the previous year. Val was a bit embarrassed for reluctantly selling the left over cards. She shared the fact she had given out most of the cards to friends but had run out of people to share them with. Val may have been embarrassed, however I was thrilled to have another connection from my precious girl!

Cheryn, Christy's Spirit Light, and Carl on our first dinner date.

The Surprised Medium

Love Calls Often, Pick up the Phone!

    I have been able to function and have actually learned to enjoy life again, because of my understanding about Life After Life, and with the help of my loving husband, Carl. He has a profound belief in God and Good and supports me in my Mediumship -- even though it is a mystery to us all!

    I'm so very thankful to have been given my perfect soul mate to love and to travel with, through the rest of this lifetime.

Cheryn Ryan

Buddy and the Light Show

This amazing occurrence happened one night, when my friend and I went to (what we thought was) a study group for <u>A Course in Miracles</u> at my church. Instead of a discussion, the plan that night was for the attendees to experience and face our deepest fears. *(Oh, well, we were already there, so we decided to stay.)*

When we walked into the meeting room, I saw lights flickering off and on. I mentioned the lights to other attendees, but no one else in the room noticed them! The facilitator began the evening by suggesting each of us try to "Face our greatest fears and overcome them."

The Surprised Medium

I decided to be stoic and I made this silent statement,

"My greatest fear is: I won't find my life's path."

Ahhhh, but that *wasn't* my greatest fear, and I quickly renamed it.

"My greatest fear is: my fear of dying, I want to know more about God."

And, **immediately** I shot up into the nighttime sky and traveled between stars and planets. I saw the Universe, in All its Glory, and I was so humbled.

After everyone returned from our "inner" adventures, and shared our experiences with the group, I saw Buddy, a man who had greeted me at church several times. I did not know him very well, at all.

Buddy had a light on his forehead. The light looked like a blazing sparkler! I was transfixed! Buddy looked like a Las Vegas magician to me. The light was above his eyes, in the middle of his forehead. It just stayed right there and glowed! I kept staring at him and was actually fearing for my life; I believed I might be dying from a stroke, because this scene was so very bizarre!

Another odd thing about this event -- I think Buddy was oblivious to the light shining from his face. He didn't act like a man who had a brightly glowing, flashing object two inches above his eyes! I also questioned why I was privileged to see this phenomenon.

This kind man had a heart attack and made his transition two weeks later.

When I learned about his passing, I called my minister and asked to meet with her. As I sat in her office, I shared some of the things that I had experienced. I told her what had transpired with Buddy, and she smiled and told me I had been given a "special gift" – that I had actually seen the *divinity* in Buddy. I cried at being told this, and I wanted to learn more.

The Surprised Medium

We talked about my self-studies and my many other visitations, and she urged me to continue studying and to share my knowledge with others, when I was ready.

Cheryn Ryan

Student of Life

At this time in my life, I became serious enough to learn more about our afterlife. I studied Spirit's messages by reading dozens of books and hundreds of articles and by watching videos of various Mediums.

One of my favorite Mediums is John Edward. I have seen him three times during the past few years. When I found out he was coming to Houston, in 2006, I ordered a ticket and went. This was just after my own father died, and I quietly asked my angels and guides to help him come through. John shared dozens of accurate messages that evening in his audience of several thousand people.

I was very pleased when John called on me *first -- "The Lady in the blue top!"* in an auditorium filled with people; He asked me

The Surprised Medium

and two other women to stand up. We all three stood and John proceeded to tell me accurate and unknown, to any others, information about my deceased mother, father, and uncle. He first said,

"Your mother said she does not like your new white carpet!"

And that would certainly be something my mom would have said about the new living room carpeting in my home!

He then told me,

"Your dad is a golfer and there's someone -- another man, who has passed, and who was close to you and your family. He's a golfer, too. They're having a good time golfing!"

"And, they're telling me, they both enjoy watching your husband, when he golfs."

Correct!

Hearing John say these things was a wonderful fulfilling experience!

Cheryn Ryan

The other women were quite surprised when he told them family information, too. He said one of the women's husband had a birthmark that resembled a burn on his arm, which John described to a "T".

He described a large barn on her family's property and mentioned activities that occur there. John told her exactly what it looked like, as she shook her head "yes" over, and over, again.

I really enjoyed seeing other people's eyes open wide, in awe, as their loved ones came to them by way of the famous, and always very accurate Medium, John Edward. For me, it was magical evening.

The Surprised Medium

"Move Over ... NOW!"

One day while driving in my hometown, and heading toward Galveston Bay, my "go-to place" when I needed to get away and drink in fresh sea air, I approached a left hand turn and I clearly heard someone shouting in my head,

"Move over ... NOW!"

I was startled and quickly complied, rapidly moving into the outer lane, as I rounded the curve. Within 50 feet, I saw a man standing by a disabled car in the inner lane — the lane, *where I had been, and the lane where I would have driven straight into him and his car!*

I slowed down and thanked God and my angels for this warning.

Cheryn Ryan

The Day I Almost Died

Another day a few months later, I had an extremely close near-death experience that still rocks my thought of "what could" have occurred.

I left my company office and headed home. I was upset with my then husband about a discussion we had just had. As, I explained, that marriage was not without problems, and our talk that particular afternoon had been exceptionally trying for both of us.

When I drove away from our company, it was the middle of the afternoon and traffic was very light. I had traveled this same road hundreds of times through the years, and I knew it like I knew my own kitchen. When I approached South Houston Road, a typical neighborhood street, the light changed to red.

The Surprised Medium

I stopped and thought back, through our heated talk. As I sat waiting for the light to change, I looked up at my mirror and to the car behind mine. I saw two men in a nondescript white sedan, and I immediately thought, *"They must be Men of God."*, and a gentle peace came over me. I decided they were, most likely, affiliated with a certain church group -- It didn't matter which group, they just made me feel so peaceful inside.

I Center Myself

and

Ask for Divine Guidance

Cheryn Ryan

The traffic light changed to green, and normally I am an aggressive driver who jumps when the signal changes, but this time I looked back into the mirror at the peaceful men and felt calm once again. I released my brake, looked right, and was going to look left, when – far off to my right, I saw a speeding car heading toward the intersection.

I braked ... held up both my hands and **screamed**,

"STOP!"

to the pick-up driver heading my way from across the street!

Luckily, he saw me, and stopped in the middle of the intersection; Then we watched as the racing car swerved and careened around him at 60 miles per hour, and barely missed hitting his truck and my car.

It was clearly obvious, the pick-up driver, the driver of that speeding car, and I miraculously avoided dying that afternoon.

The Surprised Medium

I took a deep breath, sat quietly shaking through another red light, and said a prayer of thanks to God. I finally took my foot off the brake and started on my way home. I looked into the mirror and thanked those gentlemen for exuding such peacefulness and causing me to calm down enough to clearly see the danger heading our way.

Their car followed me through the empty intersection.

Then they weren't there.

Their car did not turn -- there was no place to do so, It did not stop – The men and their car simply disappeared from sight.

Friends and After-Life Connections

After these events, I shared my thoughts and experiences with close friends and family. I received the to-be-expected replies of disbelief from some of them, and I was told some very personal and lovely stories of loved ones, who reached through the thin veil between Heaven and Earth to connect with their grieving family and friends still here.

The Surprised Medium

DaNelle

When my husband's best friend (my secret boyfriend), Ronnie died I had the strangest thing happen. It was a weekday, at 10:20 in the morning. I was at home studying for my class and my husband was at work. All of a sudden, I had a surging electrical shock run completely through my body. I'd never had anything like that happen and didn't know why, how, or what it was! I was sitting on my sofa, nowhere near a power source.

The next day, a call came in and we were told Ronnie had been killed in a farm accident the previous day around 10:20 a.m. I still think about him and the fact he came to say a final goodbye to me.

Cheryn Ryan

Deb

Deb shared her experiences of her deceased mother, who had passed when Deb was just a teenager.

"In my dreams, Mom sat on my bed and talked to me. She told me she wouldn't be here to take care of us, so she needed my help to watch over her other children. Mom continued visiting often in my dreams and often in a lovely vision of cool sheets and a gentle fan blowing over the bed, where all three of us children lay. She came to me, the very best way she could, in a way I was comforted and felt her love."

The Surprised Medium

Clifford

Three months after my dad passed, at age nine-two, he appeared in my dream. In this very lucid dream, dad was sitting about four feet from me, to the left of my position. He looked like he did when he was he was in his forties, during the 1950's -- a little heavier, and sporting his annual summer buzz haircut.

He looked so healthy and was smiling his big broad smile, like he always did in this life.

I was startled, even though I had been patiently waiting for his visit, and I said,

"Dad, what are you doing?"

He quickly replied,

"I'm learning to climb mountains!"

And, I awoke.

Cheryn Ryan

Later that morning, when I called my brother to tell him about Dad's visitation, he started laughing. I was a bit dismayed and asked what was going on. Craig replied,

"Dad was afraid of heights, didn't you know?"

I thought long and hard and realized this was something about our dad that I had never heard. I was over-joyed that he came to visit *and* gave me a bit of evidential information, I had not previously known. My sweet father was on a grand new adventure, in his new home, yet he came to share his joy with me!

*Dad,
THANK YOU,
for your love!*

Cliff and Chris Ryan, 1995

The Surprised Medium

Larry, the Owl

I must begin this vignette with the fact that we had never seen an owl on our property in the previous four years, nor since this happened.

My husband, Carl and his brother, Larry share many things in this life and beyond. These two men have a deep love for God, Jesus, their families, their country, and helping people in need. They were both athletes and played basketball, tennis, and golf together for many years, in addition to sharing their Christianity.

Larry had cancer and was dying. He was in a hospital many miles away from us and, on the days he would be without family visitors, Carl often made the seven hour round-trip to visit with him. These loving brothers talked about their past, the Bible, their families, and of course, sports. They could talk about the Houston and Dallas football teams for hours, on end.

A few days after Carl's last visit to see him, Larry's vital statistics declined late in the afternoon. At this very same time, as Carl and I were sitting on our back patio, a large owl landed in our yard, a few feet from where we sat. We had never even seen an owl here, much less during daylight hours! This beautiful, muscular, bird of prey walked around on the ground, flew up onto a tree stump, then flew to another limb and stayed in our yard, until way past dark.

The next morning, we received the call that Larry had passed. We cried and prayed all day and made plans to go back to our hometown. We walked around in a haze. This was Carl's best friend, his baby brother, and we were both so very sad.

The Surprised Medium

That afternoon, as Carl and I sat on our patio, the owl landed in our yard and did the very same thing; He walked around on the ground, flew up onto the stump, then flew to another limb. Again, he stayed until after dark.

In the past I have seen information about the sacredness of animal sightings, so I did some research on the internet for animal totems and animal meanings for current and ancestral people. I discovered:

The appearance of an owl represents the time and space between two worlds, Earth and Heaven!

The next afternoon "Larry, The Owl" came for his final visit. He landed in our back yard in the late afternoon and went through his usual routine and stayed until after dark. Both Carl and I thanked him for his appearances and said prayers for Larry's continued soul's journey.

Cheryn Ryan

We reminded him how much he is loved -- by so many people -- and how much we would miss seeing him here, however we *know* he is out of pain and on to great adventures!

The Surprised Medium

Super Mediums and Others

I joined a group of like-minded Mediums, people from all around the U.S.A., and one nice fellow in South Korea. We met online twice a month to discuss our readings, good books, online courses, and what was cooking in our kitchens. This group became a staple in my life for a long time and we dubbed ourselves the *"Super Mediums"*.

Several of our members desired to become proficient in doing readings for large groups of people; Two of our members worked on the technology needed to host such meetings, and I think another one -- or two are interested in teaching mediumship. The remainder of us work on our clarity to bring messages to our clients.

All, in all, I practiced with three different online groups and also with friends and neighbors. One night, while online, I asked the members of one of my groups to concentrate on an extremely sensational national news crime case that was on-going nearby. This was dubbed "The Austin Bomber" case and was highlighted by the indiscriminate killing of innocent people.

Nervous citizens in this area were wary of opening delivered packages and boxes and of simply going for neighborhood walks, because this killer had destroyed several lives.

People are Waiting for Good News

The Surprised Medium

Draylen

The members of my Tuesday evening Mediums group put their thoughts into this case, as did I. One of the attendees mentioned a town, just north of Austin. I don't recall any other input by the rest of them. I had a couple ideas also, but nothing quite concrete.

I decided to pursue looking into this case after class and I stayed up until 4:00 in the morning, asking Spirit to show me information that would be helpful to law enforcement. I saw the number "2" in an address and searched for 2nd or 12th streets on internet maps -- way into the wee hours. I was simply looking for a property that drew my attention.

The following day, I decided to try something I had never done before -- to communicate with one of the killer's victims, and I said a prayer for guidance and understanding -- which I always do, before a reading.

I asked the seventeen-year-old musical genius, a gentle and kind boy named Draylen, to help me. Draylen had been brutally murdered in a bomb explosion, and I hoped he would give me *any* clues, *any* information, to discover his murderer.

The young man came through quicker than I thought would happen and clearly said,

"Marco".

I asked him to describe "Marco" to me.

Draylen said,

"He is in his twenties. He is slightly built. He has brown hair. He is non-military. He is acting alone."

I asked him to give me any more information to help stop "Marco" from doing more harm.

Draylen next said,

The Surprised Medium

"He is really mixed up in his head."

I thanked Draylen for coming forward and told him I would try to help.

He replied,

"Tell my family I'm fine and I love them, very, very much!"

I shared the information I had gotten with my husband and several good friends; I told them I was not *quite sure* what I had received.

A few mornings later one of my friends called me and said,

"YOU GOT IT, CHERYN! ... YOU KNEW HIS NAME AND SOME DETAILS!"

I rushed into my living room and turned on my tv news station, to see the name "Mark Condit" blazoned across the screen. This was the man who was the subject of the nation-wide search ...he was the *Austin Bomber!*

Mark was in his twenties; Mark had a slight build; He had brown hair.

Cheryn Ryan

He acted alone; And he lived on 2nd street in a near-by town.

I cried for days. I walked around like I was lost, lost in my own home.

I didn't know what to do with this information.

I didn't know if I could pursue *things like this*, if I was going to feel *this heaviness -- this intense sadness, pouring over me!*

This discovery of communication with a deceased STRANGER -- no human client – no person, *except myself* pursuing information, was so very different for me. It presented many unanswered questions and a huge dilemma, because I think one of the tasks I'm given in this life, is to help parents whose children are missing and/or may have passed.

I also *know*, from my previous attempts to notify local police and national FBI offices -- *they may not be open to a "Medium"* contacting them about their pending cases!

The Surprised Medium

I had previously called different states Sheriffs offices and the FBI about two missing, presumed abducted girls. I had, what I thought, was valid information for each of these cases. I spoke with an officer involved in one of the "cold" cases, but did not receive communication from him after our initial contact.

I never heard back from the officers who took my information in the other missing girl case, either -- the one case, in which I believed the child to still be alive; Thank God, that young girl was found a few months later, when she was able to escape from her abductor.

At this stage of my life, I'm leaving my options as a Psychic Detective open, and will see what happens. However, I'd really ... *really* appreciate a message from Great Spirit, shouting ...

Cheryn Ryan

"RING-A-DING! RING-A-DING! THIS IS YOUR PATH, CHERYN!"

The Surprised Medium

Client's Readings

When a Medium gives information from a loved one in Spirit to a person, it is called a "Reading", perhaps because some Mediums write while doing the reading. Often, I scribble down words or names from the impressions and messages that I feel, hear, or see.

The information I receive from Spirit comes through as words, phrases, or songs I hear, or through my memory bank of pictures and things I have seen. The client is called a "Sitter" -- I suppose that's because the client sits in front of the Medium. (Funny, I had never thought of this as strange, but it does sound a bit unusual.)

Through trial and error, I *know* my role ...

I am here to serve Spirit and relay their messages and information.

Spirit People are my *real* clients, and their loved ones, are the message recipients.

Every single time I give a reading to someone, I am in total awe of Great Spirit, and the love that shines through the veil between this life and Heaven.

When my clients sit down, I explain my role as "Middle Person"; And, as they await their messages, I pray for clarity and the understanding to repeat them.

I strive to receive all information correctly and clearly, and to be the best helper to Spirit People who have reached out to me in trust and faith.

The Surprised Medium

Dear Holy Spirit, Bring Your Messages

I don't usually "see" people standing in front of me, like some other Mediums do. Frequently, I get a sense of how they looked or what their personality had been. For the most part, I "see" *my own memories* -- my memory bank of people and situations I've known and experienced. I see movies, tv shows, and plays I watched at some time during my life. I hear songs I have enjoyed. I see the titles of books I've read.

I hear my guides talking to me. I receive their signals in bits and pieces -- like a puzzle some times, and at other times, it's as if they are on a loud speaker booming words in my ear!

It is often up to my sitter to figure out the puzzling information I've offered.

Again, sometimes the messages come through loud and clear to me and my sitter, and other times we have to consider different scenarios. For instance, if I see George Washington, I may think a name is George ... or he lived in Washington ... or he taught American History! Other times Spirit People are very clear, and I'll know exactly what they are communicating.

A few people have asked me, if being a Medium is scary.

The questions go further,

"What about really bad people, or people who were murdered, are they frightening?"

The very first time a Spirit Person told me they had been murdered, I was startled *(definitely a "human" response)*. When I settled down, I found there was no difference in the way they presented their story to me and the way others, who died from natural causes, did. These communicators were living, Earth dwelling people before they passed. I encountered no difference in their emotions and appearance, and that of other Spirit People I've met. They simply want to communicate with humans they love; And they use me to do just that. Therefore, my response is the same –

"No. Spirt People are not scary."

I actually think Spirit People might get a chuckle from us trying to decipher the information they bring forth. I envision them doing an invisible belly laugh at our expense! More often than not, I sit in total amazement when I receive their precise, and so often intriguing, messages.

I simply love watching my sitters as they receive these messages, all lovingly sent through the invisible veil between Earth and Heaven!

Cheryn Ryan

Mediumship is a Gift from God, and my Gift to Others

When I made the decision to "go public" with my gift, I asked a number of friends from my church and from neighborhood and women's groups I was in, to allow me to give them free readings. I was completely overwhelmed at the positive responses!

This real-life practice helped me feel at ease and to become a better Medium. Very importantly, during this trial period, I also learned everybody expects different things when they sit with a Medium.

Carlene

Carlene is my friend from church and from a woman's group we enjoy together. She volunteered to sit for me, so I could practice.

I didn't know Carlene's history, except for a few things -- none of which came through during her reading. She is twenty years older than I, and I anticipated a whole different scenario with aunts and uncles and grandparents coming through.

I was not prepared for what happened and who showed up. When she got settled into her chair, all of her long passed social circle of friends started talking in my ear! These were a group of friends that met regularly to play "parlor" games, charades, bridge, etc., when Carlene was a young woman, during pre-World War II years.

One fellow, Harry came and produced a photo of a young and beautiful Carlene and asked me to say,

"Carlene, You were my Pin-Up Girl, when I was in the Navy".

Carlene verified Harry was in the Navy, yet she honestly had not known he had a crush on her, as they each had different boy and girl friends during that time.

Carlene was, quite honestly, *"blown away"*, as she reminisced with her long-ago friends. Her group, George, Betty, Harry and others told Carlene,

"Don't be pre-occupied with your health issues, just enjoy life and we'll see you when you're ready to come!"

The Surprised Medium

Kathy

Kathy is another of my friends and volunteers for my practice. She is a life-long Christian.

When Kathy walked in the door, her mother, Jeniece who had passed many years before, came in with her. She said to tell Kathy she is around her often and proceeded to describe some of the things that were happening in Kathy's life.

Jeniece brought her sister, Allie and another relative, Dan. Next, Jeniece ushered in a young male student of Kathy's, who had passed in a motorcycle accident, shortly after he left school.

Kathy and I talked for about an hour and a half, she reminiscing about the many people in her life who had crossed. We talked about the process of leaving Earth and entering

Heaven. Her belief corresponds with mine: We leave here and in an "instant", we are in Heaven, being surrounded by love and beauty.

Before we completed our visit, Kathy asked me the name of her spiritual guide, and I immediately heard a name and repeated it. Kathy was so pleased, and thanked me profusely, over and over, as she fairly shouted, *"That's IT! ... That's IT! ... I KNEW IT!"*

The Surprised Medium

Belle

Belle came to visit me one day, and asked me to connect with her family and friends. Her dad stepped up and reminded me of the 1950's and 1960's actor, Maurice Chevalier. He was quite debonair and he started talking about fires, as he struck a match. (At that time, there were on-going wild fires in their home state, of Oklahoma, which endangered some family members.) He clicked his heels and gave a "thumbs up" as he said he really liked Belle's new boyfriend. Her dad gave me more information about other relatives, a cousin, and other family friends, too. Then he sashayed away. Belle was thrilled with her reading and said everything I told her "fit".

Cheryn Ryan

Mitchell

Mitchell is one of my internet study buddies. One evening, I read for him, from thousands of miles away. I was hesitant, as this was my first "over the ocean" reading. Ha! I shouldn't have been concerned, as Mitchell's grandmother, Sally told me she had grown up in Kentucky -- just outside of town.

Sally told me her husband had been injured by strangers and he never fully recovered from "the attack". (As It turned out Mitchell's grandfather, Jack, was a train conductor and was mugged after he left a late-night job on his way home. He was left for dead, but survived with serious injuries.)

I was very happy, when Mitch told me *everything* I had shared was correct. I was hesitant to read for another Medium because

The Surprised Medium

I was afraid of not being able to receive *evidential* information to share with him, a common worry for many Mediums, I have been told. Basically, it's the fear of not connecting and of disappointing our client.

As I've said so many times, *I am always in awe of Holy Spirit's delivery system!* When I gave Mitch a lot of correct information, I had to pull my ego in and remind myself, it wasn't *me* who shared this information.

Cheryn Ryan

Lynne

Lynne is a woman I know socially. She volunteered to come for a reading with me. She came to me with an open mind and acknowledged she had visited other Mediums in the past. When she first sat down, I saw an older gentleman.

Lynne's husband was considerably older than she when he passed and he showed up immediately and told her it was ok to date other men, and even mentioned the name of one of her old boyfriends! He was telling this woman he loves, he doesn't want her to be lonely or unhappy.

Lynne's mother showed up next and showed me her apron. I thought that was just my reference for a loving mother or grandmother, but *No!* … Lynne's mom had a huge grin and pointed animatedly to her

The Surprised Medium

apron. It turned out, Lynne's mom collected aprons and Lynne has a favorite photo of her mom in one of those special aprons. *(I simply love how Spirit People carry on, most often just like they did when they had human bodies!)*

During this time, Lynne's step daughter came through loud and clear. She gave me the initials T.S., and Lynne verified those were for Terri Suzanne. She then shared how much Lynne meant to her and how pleased and very proud she was to call her, *"My Second Mom"*.

Cheryn Ryan

Mediums Help Heal Two Worlds

Jenna

Jenna was referred to me by her friend, Lynne. She sat down and I saw her as a little girl, dressed like a cherished doll. I was then shown her Aunt June, who has always been like a mother to Jenna. Spirit shared the bond these two women have for each other. Their connection has deepened through the years and June adores the "daughter she always wanted".

Next Jenna's deceased mother showed up and said,

"Everyone, shush and sit still, so I can listen to the football game!"

Jenna said her mom liked to place wagers on those games; It was important to her to be able to hear what was happening at the games by listening to the play by play on their radio.

The money from those games most likely helped the family, because Jenna's dad, Barry came next and told me he had died, when Jenna was just a teenager. He said he was so sorry he had to leave when she was so young.

Barry was a humble man, kind, and loving and he shared how proud he was of the woman Jenna had become. He asked her to always remember: He loves her.

A friend's son, Jan, came through next and showed me he had died from either a brain illness or head injury. He said to tell his dad,

"I am on new adventures; Don't worry, Dad! I'm fine!"

This same young man came through on a different reading from another friend of his father. It was a loving walk through the veil of Heaven to make sure his dad and family knew he is still around them.

Cheryn Ryan

A year later, Jenna called and asked to meet me six weeks after her loving husband, Leonard passed in an automobile accident on his way home to Jenna.

Leonard arrived in my sleep *the night before* Jenna's appointment. I was a bit surprised, as this was the first time one of my client's loved ones appeared in my sleep -- *and even before I was introduced to him!*

His message was an urgent matter to him, and he wanted to make sure I got the information loud and clear! I told Jenna, Leonard had mentioned,

"The time is wrong!"

He then proceeded to tell her,

"You, are the love of my life and I want you to always be happy."

Jenna worried that he had suffered in the accident. He said,

"I was there, then I was here.",

The Surprised Medium

indicating his transition was immediate and he did not suffer.

Jenna told me his death certificate had the wrong time of his death. It appeared Leonard wanted that changed to the correct time, to alleviate any confusion, and to prove to Jenna he was still around and watching over her.

Cheryn Ryan

Sandy

Sandy visited one day. She was referred to me by a mutual friend. I didn't know who, or what to expect, as she sat down, but ... Wow! Sandy's brother, her husband, and her father were lined up to communicate *all at once*, and I was a bit overwhelmed at first.

Her father had an unusual name and I was slowly given his name, then her brother chimed in and sharing the same name. They showed me a tall structure, like a very tall ladder that her father had worked on. I told this to Sandy, but she was unsure, until she reminded herself that he worked construction and on tall oil rigs, that do look like ladders.

I was also shown a fishing camp that was *"a very special place for our family"* and I saw a hammock, which hung in a tree at that

The Surprised Medium

camp. Sandy confirmed the camp was "a very special place" her family visited whenever they could get away for week-ends and holidays; She said they had an oversized hammock hanging on the property that got a lot of use by her dad and brother.

Next, her brother showed me a piggy bank he had given as a gift to Sandy, when she was a child. She laughed at the thought of that piggy bank and smiled at all the special attention she received that day. I learned how to ask Spirit People to *"Please take turns sharing!"*

Cheryn Ryan

Maddie

During this reading, Maddie's grandmother and grandfather, along with other family members, came through very clearly. They each gave me detailed information and family stories to relate to Maddie.

There had been a deadly automobile accident involved with one relative and Maddie confirmed that. Her little grandmother proudly showed me how she often pounded a table to get her family's attention and to make her point. Maddie laughed and said,

"Yes! She pounded the table a lot, that was the way she made things more dramatic. She liked to get our attention... That's my grandma!"

The Surprised Medium

Maddie told me everything I shared about her family was correct, and I was pleased to connect her with her loved ones.

After her very detailed reading, Maddie insisted I give her information and direction for her life's path. When I reminded her this was a reading for her loved ones, she *insisted* again. She wanted me to reveal what her future held; She wanted the perfect prediction for her unfolding life, and I had no answer -- even after I asked her unresponsive loved ones. I encouraged Maddie to find out herself, to meditate and ask her guides and angels.

I had given Maddie numerous, accurate, and verifiable messages from her loved ones. I learned from this encounter ... you *can't please everyone*.

As an aside, I have received hundreds of messages from Spirit People giving advice, as they had done when they walked the Earth, and I share those with my sitters.

Cheryn Ryan

Anne

Anne is another woman who was referred to me by a previous sitter. When Anne sat down, her mother immediately appeared and said,

"I'm sixty years old and Anne is my precious daughter, and I love her so much. She took such good care of me, and she does that with others, too. She's an angel!"

I soon realized Anne's mom developed early-stage Alzheimer's when she was sixty and Anne did help take care of her mother in her final years. Anne appreciated the words of her mother, and the love her mother offered, because she was not capable of expressing such sentiments during her last years.

The Surprised Medium

Next, a woman named Carol came into my vision. Anne said she was a dear friend who had passed at a young age.

A man, Anne's father, sat down and started reading a book. He picked up another book … then another … and another! My immediate thought was her dad was a very avid reader, but Anne explained he had been a successful book editor. He is still reading a lot of books!

Just as we were winding up our session, I saw a small black and white dog sitting next to her father. I described him to Anne, and she told me this pooch was their family dog and her dad's companion for many years. (This was the first pet I saw in Heaven, and it made me so happy!)

Cheryn Ryan

Linda, Bob, and Danny

I attended the same church as Linda and Bob. I soon learned their only child, Danny had died at a young age in an automobile accident. Linda allowed me to do a reading for her and Danny showed up loud and clear. He talked about his love for his parents, that they had been *"The Best of the Best"*, and that he is around them quite a lot.

This was confirmed by Linda, when she told me he played havoc with their computer. Danny's cartoon character graphics popped up onto the screen without her opening them. He turned on lights and sounds and both she and Bob felt Danny near very often.

Shortly after I did this reading, I was in a study group with other Student-Mediums. A Spirit Person told me to say,

The Surprised Medium

"I'm Dan, the Man".

No one responded, so I put that thought aside. Next one of my friends mentioned "A young, light-haired man, who died in an auto accident and is strutting his stuff." I didn't get the connection for another few minutes, until he said to me,

"It's Me, Danny!"

Danny's visit here was another "first" for me, the first time someone I didn't know in this life, just popped up to bring more messages to share! I'm glad it was the loving son of my friends who appeared. I soon recognized other Spirt People bringing me information, prior to an upcoming reading.

Unfortunately, our dear Bob became quite ill, and passed very quickly. One of my last meetings with a study group, brought Bob in that same "loud and clear" way as his son, Danny had previously appeared, and like Bob was in this Earth life!

Cheryn Ryan

The other members of our group did a round table reading with Linda. Bob and Danny came through and shared many sweet and funny memories.

I didn't think I would get any messages, as often happens when a Medium is close to the sitter, but I did.

Bob showed up, in a very unusual way! He appeared by pushing aside some tall bamboo plants -- like he was appearing from behind a stage (bamboo) curtain. He was holding a present, complete with big bow, which he said was *"for his Sweetheart"*.

Linda and I were both baffled! She had no idea what that appearance was about, until a couple days later when Linda called and said,

"You're not going to believe what he did! Bob ordered some bamboo dishes, we had seen on our last vacation and had them sent to me -- they just arrived for my birthday!"

The Surprised Medium

We both laughed as Bob, huge personality that he was, -- is still *"Wowing"* people from Beyond!

And, Linda? She is one intelligent, brave, believer in Life After Life! **She gets it!** She receives messages quite regularly from her loving guys and knows they are together and on great adventures.

(By the way, Danny messes with *my* lights and my computer, now!)

Prayers Reach our Loved Ones

Cheryn Ryan

Carl A.

Carl A. Is my long-time friend and was married to one of my dearest friends, Deanna. He died from cancer and I attended his memorial and stayed with Deanna for a few days afterward. I left their town, drove five hours back to my home and prepared for a long-scheduled seminar in Arizona.

When I got to the week-end seminar, I was ill with a terrible head cold I had contracted at the memorial. I felt horrible! I had pre-paid in advance for the workshop and for hotels and B and B's during this working vacation. I didn't feel I could cancel everything, so my husband and I went boldly forward!

This workshop was headed by Suzanne Giesemann, the same Medium I first studied with in-person. I felt I would not be able to

The Surprised Medium

participate fully with the other attendees, however what happened was pretty solidly incredible, in my opinion.

I had a number of practice exercises with other students, and *EVERY ONE of the students who gave me a reading, told me Carl A. was giving them information ... EVERY SINGLE ONE of them!*

One woman drew a picture of him, after fully describing him accurately. She and five other people -- separately and apart from the other readers, told me how funny he was. (Carl A. was one of the funniest friends I've ever had!)

They each said he was very tall, (6'5") and showed up wearing a cowboy hat, jeans and boots (He *always* wore them!) They all mentioned he loved dogs and horses, loved hunting and fishing, and above all, he loved his wife, daughters and family. Each one of these reports were "right on"!

These descriptions of him were just so incredibly correct, in every way. The fact he kept interjecting himself into all the exercises was just so very much "Carl A." to me! He was the proverbial "Life of the Party" and these were fantastic experiences for me, even though I was feeling ill, and still very sad he had transitioned. That wonderful guy did not disappoint!

The Surprised Medium

Hannah

Hannah and I had a session on the internet. Her brother popped right in and Hannah was confused. Jon, Hannah's brother told me he is *"still here, but there, as well"*, and I understood. Jon is in an assisted living residence because he suffers from advanced dementia. He said,

"Most of the time I am already in Heaven".

"Please don't squander your time on me, I'm ok. I really wish I were more like you, Hannah. I love you, Sis, you're the best!"

As he pulled back, Hannah's son came through. He was riding a motorcycle and loves doing so. He said his "Grand Pop" was with him and they "look alike" -- both very dashing -- in their *overalls!*

Cheryn Ryan

Hannah's mother showed up and said she is really "cutting loose"! She was wearing a boa and had a short bob haircut. Hannah's son agreed with his grandmother by touching his index finger to the tip of his nose, meaning that's right on -- that's correct! *("Right On" and a gentle touch to one's nose is a signal I receive often from my guides and Spirit People.)*

Hannah is a very spiritual person who understands our loved ones live on in another dimension. She said everything I told her was correct, down to the old black and white photo of her mother with a short bob haircut and wearing a boa!

Jennifer

Jennifer (Jenny) is another one of my "guinea pigs" and good friends. I knew her parents had died long ago, but I knew nothing else about her family history.

After Jenny sat down, I Immediately saw the name Bradly and heard a man, her father, singing a song from long ago, "Jeannie with the light brown hair." He said he loved singing that to her when she was a baby, even though he couldn't "carry a tune in a paper sack".

Jenny's mom showed up and said she loved preparing meals for her family, and loves the woman Jen has become. She showed me a suburban home and said,

"Look at my brick house, I'm so proud!

Jenny's brother, Brad stepped through and said,

"Well, I'll be darn! ... I didn't believe in this stuff before I left, but I sure do now!"

After her reading, Jenny told me her mother was really proud to have her first "Brick" home during her marriage to Jenny's father, Bradley; And Jenny confirmed: Brother Brad *did not believe* in an after-life ... *Now he knows better!*

The Surprised Medium

Adora

Adora met me online one evening. I knew she was related to a friend of mine, but knew nothing else. I felt a little bit "off", because I was experiencing an aggravating headache that day; I really hoped I could be of service to her and to her loved ones, even though I felt *"crummy"*.

I heard and saw *nothing* for a few minutes, then I did something I had not done previously during a reading; I told Adora I wasn't receiving anything and asked if she felt comfortable giving me the name of someone she wanted to hear from.

She gave me the name "Sarah" ... and *immediately* I saw Sarah.

Sarah was a young, pretty woman and she was literally dancing all around the room. She told me she and Adora "shared" something special – they had a very special bond.

Sarah showed me how she had passed; She was alone in her car and driving home in an isolated area. Her car crashed into a small ravine and she passed immediately.

Adora acknowledged everything I told her was correct. She said Sarah was a professional dancer and the "special bond" they shared is their son. Adora is stepmother to Sarah's son. She told me Sarah was a good mom and the two women got along quite well.

Sarah then said,

"Please tell everyone to look for me in the clouds."

Adora looked puzzled for a minute, then she started laughing as she told me,

The Surprised Medium

"Oh my gosh, Cheryn! Everyone who attended Sarah's memorial service wore a T-shirt with beautiful clouds on them and a picture of Sarah in the very center!"

Angels Appreciate Our Assistance

Cheryn Ryan

Connie and Nolan

Connie has become a friend through her son, Nolan. The first time she visited me, he came in like a showman. He told me his death was of his choosing, and he was so sorry to hurt his mother and other people he loves.

Nolan said he was greeted by relatives who had died years before he passed. He also talked about his maternal grandmother and a good friend of his, who both passed after he did.

He described his love for Connie and said,

"My mom is The Very BEST Mom in the World! All my friends love her, too!"

He talked at length about his friends and about his home being "the" gathering place

The Surprised Medium

for them all – and, all because of his Mother's love!

Sensitive, lovely Nolan went on and on, saying he wished his mom would not be sad. He wants Connie to know that he loves her, and *always will*. He asked her to set out more pictures of him, pictures of him smiling, and for her to know that's how he wants her to think of him -- every day,

"*Because she thinks of me Every Day, and I am right there with her!*"

Cheryn Ryan

Pam

Pam came to visit and her husband showed up right away. Jim appeared as an athlete. He told me he was "rather intelligent" and showed me Jack Nicklaus, indicating he was, at one time, a top-notch golfer. Pam laughed, saying he was quite a jokester, that he was a good golfer, but not *that* accomplished! He held up his thumb to say "right on!".

Jim showed me a banana and pointed at its shape. I didn't know what that meant, until Pam told me her loving, and funny husband suffered from debilitating bone disease in his later years, and his body was, indeed "shaped like a banana".

He said to tell her, he sometimes moves the paintings on the wall, to remind her he's "hanging around" and loves her dearly. (We

The Surprised Medium

all laughed at his joke! "Hanging around and Hanging things on the wall, too!) It's obvious, Jim carried his sense of humor with him into Heaven, even to the point of poking fun at his illness!

Next, Jim said his sisters -- all six of them -- and he, were "Hanging out in Heaven together ... doing *just* fine and having fun!"

Lastly, this loving husband finished up by telling his beloved wife,

"My Darlin', Take two of your friends and go on a tour though Europe. You need to travel."

Pam said that was *exactly* what he said to her before he passed.

(What a guy! I simply love Jim!)

Cheryn Ryan

Laura

Laura called one day and asked if I could fit her in, as soon as possible. I had a cancellation two days later and set up the appointment to see her, in place of the other person.

The first Spirit Person to show up was her mother, Mary. Next her father, Joe came in, playing a guitar. Her grandmother came in as a flapper, from the 1920's. (It was as if a door opened and they all walked in, hand in hand.)

A man appeared and said "Bear". I assumed (not necessarily a good thing for a Medium to do) he was referring to an animal or a location -- like Bear Mountain. Laura soon said that was the name of one of her former boyfriends. She had not heard from him or knew if he had passed, as it had been many years since they had spoken.

The Surprised Medium

Next, Laura's mother stepped up and shouted,

"Do <u>not</u> hesitate! ... Do it NOW!"

And Laura knew exactly what she meant.

I did not know, until Laura told me, she had been urged by her physicians to have surgery right away, and she really wanted to know which was her best option.

She trusts Spirit, and with her mother stepping up and recommending she go ahead, Laura had her answer.

(By the way, she did have that surgery and is now very healthy! ... *Yay Mom!*)

Cheryn Ryan

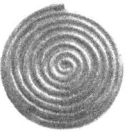

Claude

Claude was another person for whom I held a long-distant reading, via the internet. His natural languages are Spanish and French. His halting English was filled with a distinctive accent, and I was concerned about my ability to help with his concerns. I should have known better; Spirit is without limitations regarding language, communication, and distance.

Claude's grandmother, Maria, appeared and was holding a baby. She said Claude and his wife had lost a child in infancy and that precious babe was there with her. Next, I saw the familiar reference *"RIP"* and, at first, my thoughts went to someone who had recently passed.

The Surprised Medium

After the *RIP* appeared, I saw a long and winding river and was told it was in Peru. Claude's dad, Pablo, who had died many years ago, showed me he lived by a river in Peru –

(What??) "RIP" meant "River in Peru"!

Pablo also showed me the state of California and said Claude's only son lives there. He said they had always been very close, but hadn't been together for several years and they would be visiting with each other soon. Claude expressed his gratitude and told me everything I had said was true and he was so glad his father, mother, and baby had come for a visit!

I Attract Divine Guidance

Cheryn Ryan

Tamara

Tamara was in tears when we met. She told me she was very emotional and very excited about "having a meeting with her loved ones in Heaven". Tamara's family did not disappoint!

First her mother, next her father, then her sister showed up, almost simultaneously! Her sister, Karen told me she had passed from brain cancer and Tamara was her loving caretaker at the end of her Earth life.

Karen shared information about her many travels with Tamara. Their mother told me Tamara is an organic gardener and "super-good cook". Her father and other members stepped up and shared sweet memories with her. Tamara agreed everything I relayed was correct. She told me she was thinking about developing her intuitive gifts, too. I hope so,

The Surprised Medium

Tamara has a built-in support team and I believe she's a wonderful person. If she does pursue her Spiritual Path, I think she'll be a great asset to the Spirit World and us, here.

Cheryn Ryan

Casey

Casey and Ann, husband and wife, came to see me. As they settled into their chairs I instantly saw his mother falling to the floor! She told me she had a "bad fall" and never recovered from the broken hip and broken foot she sustained. Casey agreed that's exactly what had happened.

Lindy, his mom then did something quite humorous – she stood up very straight and curtsied to Queen Elizabeth! Next, she pulled out the Union Jack flag and started whirling around and singing "Hail to the Queen"! *(She was quite a good singer!)*

Casey laughed and told me his "Mum" was born in Liverpool and was extremely loyal to her native England and to the sovereignty. He said -- even growing up in the States, he enjoyed tea time every day with his parents and other relatives, all compliments of his British mother.

Casey's son, Randall, appeared at a distance, and this indicated a break in their relationship to me. Randall said they were "separated" when he passed. He said he did not hold a grudge against his father for leaving him and his mom, and in spite of that fact, he still loves his father.

Next, a close friend of Ann's, a young woman named Savannah showed up; She asked Casey and Anne to contact her mother and share her love and her continued closeness with her family. She urged them to be open to her visits and she wanted them all to know: she was *"just fine ... and as close as a whisper!"*

Cheryn Ryan

An excerpt from <u>Reaching Through the Veil to Heal</u> by Linda Drake

"For a parent, grief is painfully frightening and overwhelming with the death of a child. With suicide, the grief is compounded, as there are even more emotions attached to the seemingly senseless loss. Here is another mother's story.

Being the mom of a wonderfully loving caring, and creative young woman, I question daily her choice of suicide. Knowing she believed strongly that we go on to the next phase of our chosen path after we leave here is what sustains me, and, I believe, that belief is what allowed her to take her own life.

Suicide is not the answer and suicide is not painless, as the popular M*A*S*H television theme song says – just ask any person who has had a loved on take their own life. Suicide is painful and keeps on giving that pain to those who loved the person and are left behind. It leaves gaping holes where our hearts reside. It is the most painful thing. It does not solve the problems; it is only a way to avoid dealing with them on this plane. It leaves daily, hourly questions. It ends our ability to make hurts "better".

Do I believe my daughter and God intended her life to end early? Yes. I believe she was to have died

The Surprised Medium

in a flood three years earlier, but hundreds of prayers saved her life that long night. I believe she had come so close to death that she knew she was to have gone then. For many reasons, the following years were so sad for her that she decided to take her life.

How do I survive now without her? I pray, I meditate, and I strive to be an instrument of God's creativity, love, and light. I have had visits from her that have helped me cope. I have seen her in my dreams and know she was the reason for the ringing phone with no one there. I have closed my eyes and held her and stroked her hair. I have questioned her and had answers given almost immediately. When I am overwhelmed with tears and feel I cannot go on, I feel her presence. I see rainbows and I know that God does not offer these for no reason. I know she's gone on to continue her good work. I know."

Cheryn Ryan,

Christy's Mom

Cheryn Ryan

About my Christy, she was incredibly beautiful -- which added its own problems about the sincerity of people in her life. She was always such a sensitive soul, even as a very young child. Her bio dad was a true introvert, as were his parents. He was an only child, as were they, and Christy was the only grandchild on that side of her family.

The Surprised Medium

Recently, with the help of DNA research, I was able to discover the fact that members of Christy's paternal family suffered from depression and there were several suicides in their family, prior to hers.

I am *extremely* thankful for this knowledge and to learn about the genetics, and predisposition to depression, running through Christy's father's family.

I *urge* other parents with sensitive children to do research into their family health history, which might uncover family depression, and to seek medical help for their child, if needed.

Cheryn Ryan

Miracles, Mystery, and Mediumship

During my time as a professional Medium, I have seen, heard, and felt, so many varied, surprising, incredible, and loving messages.

How does this occur?

I "see" a memory that is connected to my sitter. For example, I saw my grandmother preparing applesauce for me and knew immediately Beau's grandmother loved him and had been a significant person in his life.

I hear music I love or I grew up with, which are given as clues to my sitter's life. *(Recall: Jenny's dad sang "Jeannie, With the Light Brown Hair" to her, when she was a child.)* Many times, I have heard the Mamas and Papas or Frank Sinatra singing in my head, Elvis has been there, too! And, offered *specifically for me,* the numerous times I've heard: Unchained Melody, Stardust, My Girl, and Danny Boy. That reaches well into the thousands. As I've mentioned before, my guides talk to me, sometimes shout at me, when I need to pay particular attention to something.

When there is a strong emotion or severe pain associated with a Spirit Person, I may get an uncomfortable feeling. I have briefly felt some of their sadness, regret, exhilaration, exhaustion, happiness, and any array of emotions.

I'm usually shown the problem area of the Spirt Person's body that affected their health and perhaps was the ultimate cause of their passing. I have been told by several Spirit People how they were murdered. (I was really surprised at that declaration, and the understanding they did not appear angry. *They simply stated a fact.)* I have learned the pain associated with such a passing is left here, and *not* carried into Heaven, a very comforting realization for me and others.

Many times, I have received information from Spirit which my sitter doesn't understand. I always urge my client to remember this message and to keep an open mind about this subject. More times than not, my sitter will contact me at a later date to tell me they "get" it, now!

Every single time I do a reading – *EVERY SINGLE TIME*, I sit in Awe of this incredible life we have; I sit in awe of our Great Spirit!

I am so privileged to be the Broker, the Middle Person, the Medium, as I am allowed the honor to *truly, honestly, see and feel the love* shared between our two worlds!

My Spiritual Beliefs

Thankfully we can dispose of those "boogey man" threats of a fiery place called Hell and the fantastic gold and jewel packed Heaven. We know we are all together, with God!

As a Christian, I follow Jesus' teachings, and YES, I still call the next world, "Heaven". *(Habit, I guess... and I look forward to angels and Jesus greeting us in the next phase of our lives; Don't you?)*

I know other prophets have shared their light around this world as Jesus did, and they also taught people to love one another as we love ourselves. Our goal, our path here is to serve our sisters and brothers and to accomplish good deeds, while our Souls grow to encompass that Perfect Light of Love.

Cheryn Ryan

Jesus said,

"Seek ye first the Kingdom of God and all things shall be added unto you."

and

"The Kingdom of God is within you."

It is my belief, we evolve and exist to expand our Soul and we *all* transcend into a loving existence of consciousness -- the Light, where we heal and learn before going on to a higher realm.

We are One in Spirit, One in Soul

*Lights blink on and off.

*Music plays by itself.

*Objects move and mementos appear.

*People reach out, unexpectedly to share stories about our loved ones.

*Voices and visions enter our minds.

*Special Scents fill our hearts with joy.

BELIEVE!

You are Loved, So Very Loved

There is No End to Life

There is No End to Love

www.ingramcontent.com/pod-product-compliance
Lightning Source LLC
Chambersburg PA
CBHW061313110426
42742CB00012BA/2170